Inflation
IN INFOGRAPHICS

Christina Hill

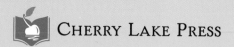

Published in the United States of America by Cherry Lake Publishing Group
Ann Arbor, Michigan
www.cherrylakepublishing.com

Reading Adviser: Beth Walker Gambro, MS, Ed., Reading Consultant, Yorkville, IL

Photo Credits: © Cover, Page 1: ©z_wei/Getty Images; Page 5: ©Cheremuha/Getty Images, ©Ihor Reshetniak/Getty Images; Page 9: ©AlexZel/Pixabay, ©Clker-Free-Vector-Images/Pixabay, ©OpenClipart-Vectors/Pixabay; Page 10: ©sorbetto/Getty Images, ©Creativa Images/Shutterstock, ©Macrovector/Shutterstock, ©NWM/Shutterstock, ©SurfsUp/Shutterstock; Page 11: ©Vadi Fuoco/Shutterstock; Page 13: ©Ja_inter/Getty Images, ©sorbetto/Getty Images, ©BRO.vector/Shutterstock, ©Irina/Shutterstock,: ©LanKogal/Shutterstock; Page 14: ©Rudzhan Nagiev/Getty Images,©Pixabay; Page 18: ©Graphics by N.D.Fernandez/Getty Images; Page 19: ©NPaveIN/Getty Images, ©FGC/Shutterstock, ©Sira Anamwong/Shutterstock; Page 20: ©Carlos Insignares/Pixabay, ©Clker-Free-Vector-Images/Pixabay, ©Megan Rexazin/Pixabay, ©Mohamed Hassan/Pixabay, ©OpenClipart-Vectors/Pixabay, ©Ricarda Mölck/Pixabay; Page 21: ©Clker-Free-Vector-Images/Pixabay, ©vidityas/Shutterstock; Page 22: ©BRO Vector/Getty Images, ©Dzm1try/Shutterstock, ©Golden Sikorka/Shutterstock, ©Microba Grandioza/Shutterstock, ©pathdoc/Shutterstock, ©Seahorse Vector/Shutterstock, ©sub job/Shutterstock, ©SurfsUp/Shutterstock; Page 23: ©OpenClipart-Vectors/Pixabay; Page 27: ©GraphicMama-team/Pixabay; Page 28: ©Mohamed Hassan/Pixabay, ©TeraVector/Shutterstock; Page 30: ©Mironova Iuliia/Shutterstock

Cherry Lake Press is an imprint of Cherry Lake Publishing Group.

Library of Congress Cataloging-in-Publication Data
Names: Hill, Christina, author.
Title: Inflation in infographics / Christina Hill.
Description: Ann Arbor, Michigan : Cherry Lake Press, [2023] | Series: Econo-graphics | Includes bibliographical references and index. | Audience: Ages 9-13 | Audience: Grades 4-6 | Summary: "Inflation is an economic issue that affects all consumers when prices for goods and services start to rise. In this book, readers will learn about the causes and effects of inflation. Large-scale and real-life examples of inflation are also presented, including facts about pandemic-era impacts. Colorful and clear graphics, such as maps, charts, and infographics, give readers an alternative to text-heavy sources. Action-based activities will leave students with ideas for how inflation affects their lives. This book also includes a glossary, index, suggested reading and websites, and a bibliography"-- Provided by publisher.
Identifiers: LCCN 2022016813 (print) | LCCN 2022016814 (ebook) | ISBN 9781668909959 (hardcover) | ISBN 9781668911556 (paperback) | ISBN 9781668914731 (pdf)
Subjects: LCSH: Inflation (Finance)--Juvenile literature. | Economics--Juvenile literature.
Classification: LCC HG229 .H549 2023 (print) | LCC HG229 (ebook) | DDC 332.4/1--dc23/eng/20220413
LC record available at https://lccn.loc.gov/2022016813
LC ebook record available at https://lccn.loc.gov/2022016814

Cherry Lake Publishing Group would like to acknowledge the work of the Partnership for 21st Century Learning, a Network of Battelle for Kids. Please visit *http://www.battelleforkids.org/networks/p21* for more information.

Printed in the United States of America

Before embracing a career as an author, **Christina Hill** received a bachelor's degree in English from the University of California, Irvine, and a graduate degree in literature from California State University, Long Beach. When she is not writing about various subjects from sports to economics, Christina can be found hiking, mastering yoga handstands, or curled up with a classic novel. Christina lives in sunny Southern California with her husband, two sons, and beloved dog, Pepper Riley.

CONTENTS

What Is Inflation?

Inflation is a rise in price over time. It usually happens when the amount of money available increases. This means that the value of money decreases as the prices of goods and services go up. When goods or services are in high **demand**, or there is a lot of money in **circulation**, customers are willing to pay more. This raises prices.

Deflation is the opposite of inflation. Prices fall because there are too many goods and services available to purchase or not enough money in circulation. If customers refuse to pay higher prices, then the prices will fall.

Inflation vs. Deflation

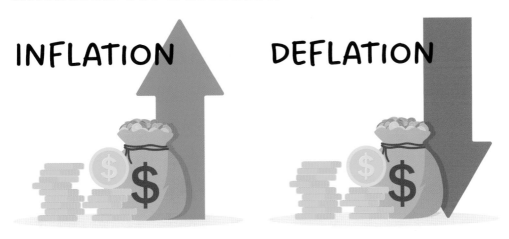

INFLATION

DEFLATION

Rising Cost of a Movie Ticket

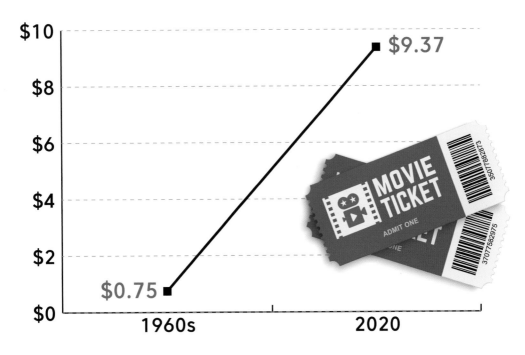

$9.37

$0.75

1960s

2020

2019, National Association of Theater Owners; 2020, Statista

Inflation and the Average Cost of a McDonald's Big Mac

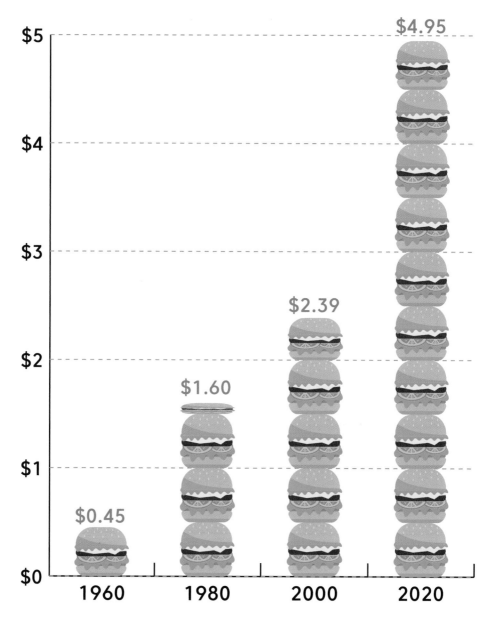

$5 —

$4 —

$3 —

$2 —

$1 —

$0 —

$4.95

$2.39

$1.60

$0.45

1960   1980   2000   2020

2020, *Eat This, Not That!*

Varying Costs of a Big Mac Across the United States (2021)

Inflation rates vary across the country. The same burger costs more depending on the region.

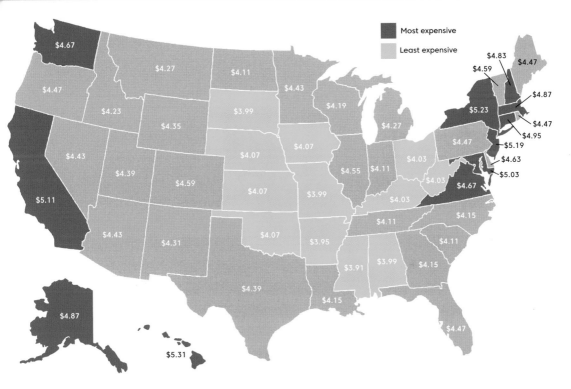

Most expensive

Least expensive

Cost Factors

- **Real estate prices**
- **Employment rates**
- **Spending habits**
- **Product availability**

2021, Fast Food Menu Prices

CHAPTER 1

Cost-Push Inflation

There are different kinds of inflation. Sometimes prices increase because the costs of **raw materials** and **wages** for workers go up. This is called cost-push inflation. The higher production costs can decrease the **supply**, but the demand for goods stays the same. The cost increases are paid for by customers in the form of higher prices.

Cost-Push Inflation

The cost of raw materials goes up.

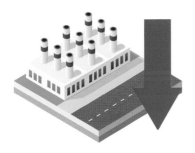

Factories have fewer materials, so production goes down.

Customers still demand the same amount.

The increased costs are passed on to the customer as higher prices.

Five Causes of Cost-Push Inflation

MONOPOLY
One company controls most of one product or service.

WAGE INFLATION
People receive an increase in the amount they earn for jobs.

NATURAL DISASTERS
Natural disasters destroy production plants or deplete a natural resource.

GOVERNMENT REGULATION
Taxes can lower demand for certain products and raise prices.

EXCHANGE RATES
If the **exchange rate** for foreign money falls, **imported** goods will cost more.

The 1973 Oil Crisis

- In 1973, the Organization of Petroleum Exporting Countries (OPEC) declared an **embargo**, or ban, on selling oil to a select group of countries. These countries included the United States, the Netherlands, Portugal, and South Africa. As a result, the price of a barrel of oil skyrocketed. This is an example of cost-push inflation.

- From 1973 to 1974, the price of a barrel of oil grew from $3 to $12. Oil prices jumped 134%.

- Gas for automobiles comes from oil. The average price of 1 gallon (3.8 liters) of regular gasoline rose 43%, from $0.385 in May 1973 to $0.551 in June 1974.

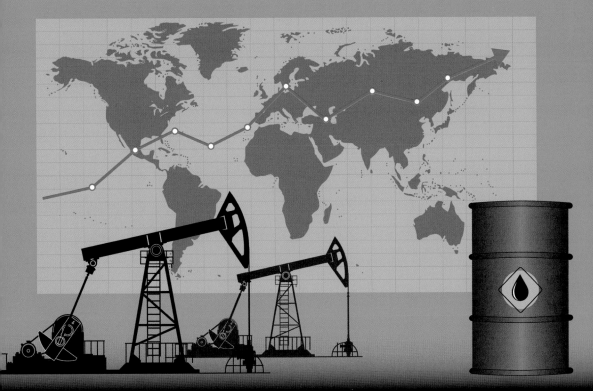

CHAPTER 2

Demand-Pull Inflation

Demand-pull inflation is when prices rise due to a sudden increase in demand and a shortage in supply. This happens when there is too much money and too few goods for sale. One good thing about demand-pull inflation is that it usually happens when there is a low unemployment rate. This means people have jobs and more money to spend. Their demand for goods and services goes up.

Five Causes of Demand-Pull Inflation

GROWING ECONOMY
Consumers feel confident and spend more money.

INCREASED FOREIGN DEMAND
If consumers buy fewer imports, but **exports** increase, prices will rise, especially if there is a difference in the exchange rate.

GOVERNMENT SPENDING
If the government increases spending, the demand for the goods it is purchasing goes up, as does the price.

INFLATION EXPECTATIONS
Companies anticipate inflation rates and raise their prices to match.

EXPANDED MONEY SUPPLY
More money in circulation with fewer goods to buy raises prices.

Consumer Demand for PlayStation 5 Inflates Prices

- The demand for PS5 gaming consoles increased during the 2020 COVID-19 pandemic. More people were staying home, and the demand for video games increased. Stores sold out of the systems within seconds. The manufacturer could not make enough to keep up with the demand.

- As a result, people began buying and reselling PS5s. The prices inflated due to the low supply and increased demand.

- Disc Version: $499; resold for $798.05; a 59.95% markup

- Digital Version: $399; resold for $759.22; a 90.28% markup

2021, ParseHub

Apple's iPhone Prices

The Apple brand is demanded by consumers, which inflates the price of each new phone that is released. This is an example of demand-pull inflation.

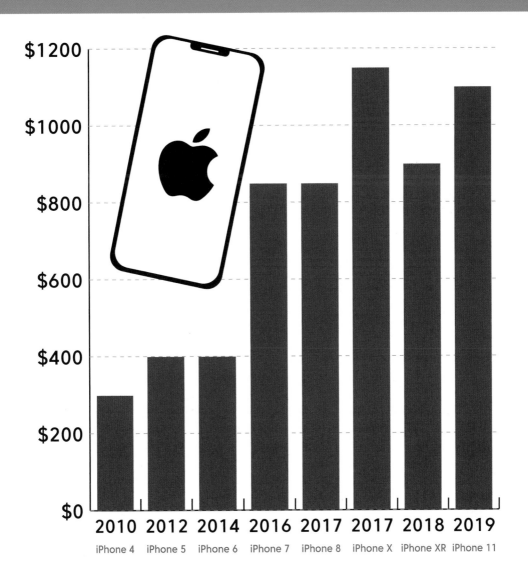

2010	2012	2014	2016	2017	2017	2018	2019
iPhone 4	iPhone 5	iPhone 6	iPhone 7	iPhone 8	iPhone X	iPhone XR	iPhone 11

2019, Apple

CHAPTER 3

Measures of Inflation

One way to track inflation is by a price index. This is a chart that measures the prices of goods and services over time.

The Consumer Price Index (CPI) measures the price of goods and services bought by consumers every month. The CPI gives people an idea about price changes, the state of the economy, and how much purchasing power a dollar has.

Unlike the CPI, the Producer Price Index (PPI) measures price changes from the seller. The PPI can predict inflation. If the cost to produce an item increases, the price will likely go up too.

The U.S. Consumer Price Index (1950-2020)

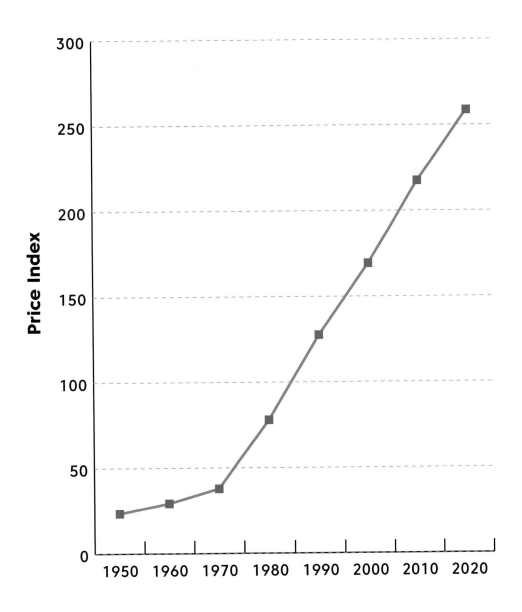

2022, U.S. Bureau of Labor Statistics

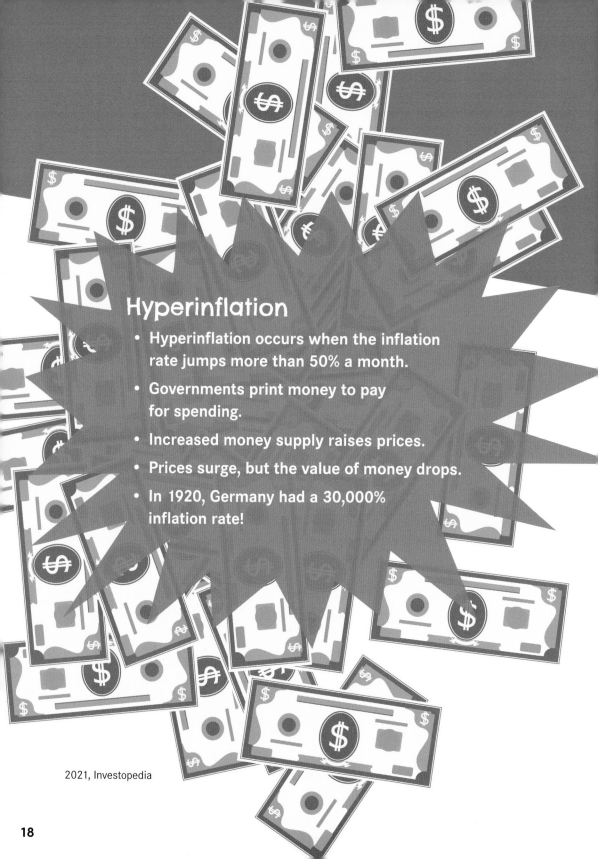

Hyperinflation

- Hyperinflation occurs when the inflation rate jumps more than 50% a month.

- Governments print money to pay for spending.

- Increased money supply raises prices.

- Prices surge, but the value of money drops.

- In 1920, Germany had a 30,000% inflation rate!

2021, Investopedia

Stagflation

Stagflation happens when there are rising prices but also high unemployment.

In the 1970s, the United States had a period of stagflation. Oil prices were high, and shipping costs soared. The high level of unemployment plus higher prices of goods caused an economic downturn, or **recession**.

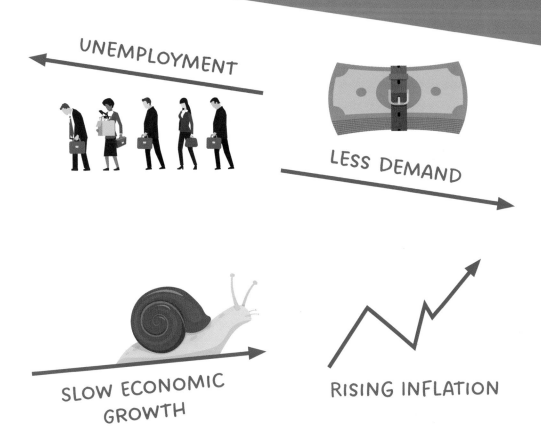

UNEMPLOYMENT

LESS DEMAND

SLOW ECONOMIC GROWTH

RISING INFLATION

Parts of the Consumer Price Index (CPI)

THE 8 MAJOR GROUPS OF THE CONSUMER PRICE INDEX

- Housing
- Apparel
- Food and Beverages
- Transportation
- Medical Care
- Education and Communication
- Recreation
- Other Goods and Services

The CPI Formula

A market basket is a set of items consumers often purchase in each of the major CPI groups. The prices of those items are tracked over time to measure inflation.

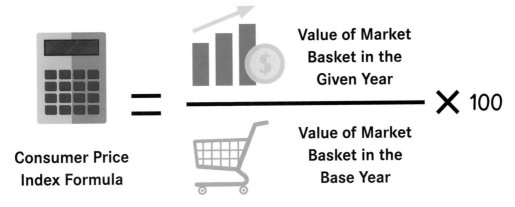

Consumer Price Index Formula $=$ $\dfrac{\text{Value of Market Basket in the Given Year}}{\text{Value of Market Basket in the Base Year}} \times 100$

CPI Formula Example

How much does it cost to make spaghetti in 2020 versus 2000?

2000	2020
Noodles: $0.60	Noodles: $1.00
Sauce: $2.00	Sauce: $3.00
Cheese: $3.00	Cheese: $4.00
The Market Basket Total: $5.60	The Market Basket Total: $8.00

(Prices for illustrative purposes only)

Answer: $8.00 divided by $5.60 is equal to $1.42; multiplied by 100 is 142. Then subtract the baseline 100 to find the percentage. 142–100 = 42% change in price.

Producer Price Index (PPI) Industries

MINING

The PPI for mining increased from 10.8% in April to 21.7% in May 2021.

MANUFACTURING

FORESTRY

FISHING

PPI INDUSTRIES

AGRICULTURE

The farm-level price received by producers for cattle rose 8.7% from January to August 2021.

NATURAL GAS AND ELECTRICITY

CONSTRUCTION

WASTE AND SCRAP MATERIALS

Fast Facts

- There are separate PPI reports for more than 535 individual industries and 4,000 products.
- The U.S. Bureau of Labor Statistics releases approximately 10,000 PPIs every month.

2022, USDA

The Federal Reserve Toolbox

The Federal Reserve is the central bank of the United States. It has a special job to control inflation.

The Federal Reserve raises interest rates when inflation is too high. Consumers begin to save and not spend as much money because it costs more to borrow.

The Federal Reserve has the right to set the reserve requirements. This is the amount of money required to be in bank vaults at all times.

The Federal Reserve sells government bonds on the open market, which takes money out of circulation.

The Value of a U.S. Dollar (1800-2020)

$1 in 1800 is equal in purchasing power to about $22.06 today.

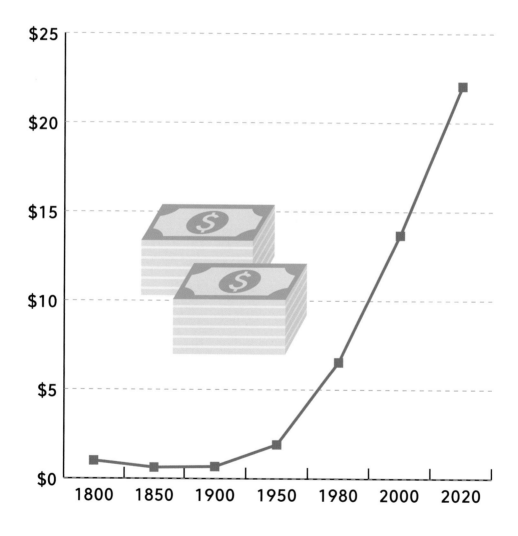

2022, CPI Inflation Calculator

Inflation Rates Around the World (2021)

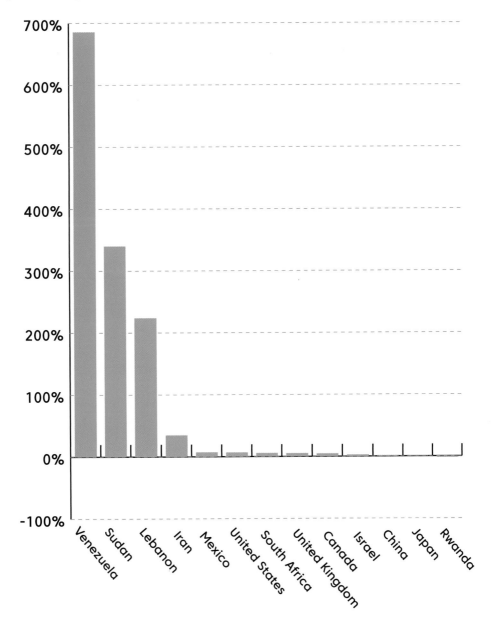

2022, Trading Economics

CHAPTER 4

Inflation Positives and Negatives

While it may seem like prices rising over time is a bad thing, there are pros and cons to inflation. Governments want a low, slow, and steady inflation rate of around 2 percent. That number indicates the economy is healthy. More dollars in circulation means more consumers with extra cash. This leads to an increase in demand and production.

People who owe money can benefit from inflation too. They can pay back what they owe more easily. In other words, the dollar is more valuable than it was when they borrowed it.

The Good and Bad of Inflation

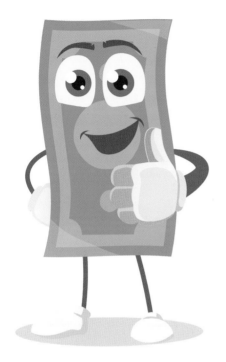

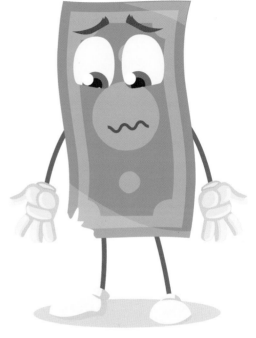

PROS

Economic growth

Adjustment of wages

Adjustment of prices

Less chance of recession

CONS

Higher cost of goods and services

Unemployment rates may rise

Cash value is decreased

If wages aren't adjusted, people receive less money for their work

Inflation Con: Higher Cost of Goods

This family spends $100 on groceries each week.

Next year, the same family fills their cart with the same items from the same store. But this time the clerk says the total is $105. The family may choose to put back an item or pay the extra $5.

5%

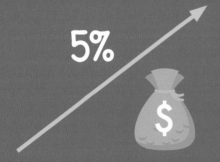

The increase in price is equal to a 5% inflation rate.

The same goods that once cost $100 are now $105, even though nothing else has changed.

U.S. Inflation Rates (2011–2021)

Inflation rates jumped after the COVID-19 pandemic began in 2020. Prices increased due to an imbalance in supply and demand.

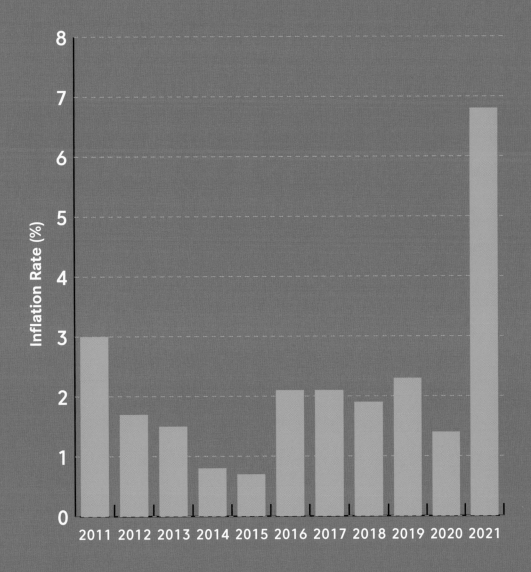

2022, U.S. Inflation Calculator

Activity

Calculate the Inflation Rate

You are wondering how much your favorite chocolate bar has increased in price over time.

Create a bar graph with the following data:

1930: $0.05

1940: $0.05

1950: $0.10

1980: $0.25

2000: $0.75

2010: $0.85

2020: $1.00

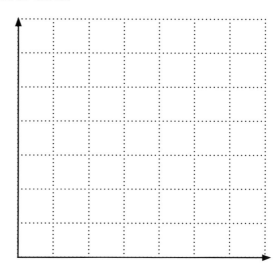

You learn that the chocolate bar was first sold in 1920, but you don't have data for that year. What is a good guess for how much it cost then?

If the inflation rate in 2021 is 3 percent, how much will you pay for your chocolate bar?

Do you think the price will always go up? Why or why not?

What might make the price of the chocolate bar fall?

Learn More

Books

Dakers, Diane. *Getting Your Money's Worth.* New York, NY: Crabtree Publishing Company, 2017.

Sebree, Chet'la. *Understanding Inflation.* New York, NY: Cavendish Square, 2020.

Websites

Britannica Kids: Inflation
https://kids.britannica.com/students/article/inflation/275058

Kiddle: Inflation Facts for Kids
https://kids.kiddle.co/Inflation

Bibliography

Dolasia, Meera. "Why Venezuelans Are Paying Millions of Bolivars for a Cup of Coffee." August 27, 2018. https://www.dogonews.com/2018/8/27/why-venezuelans-are-paying-millions-of-bolivars-for-a-cup-of-coffee

PBS Learning Media. "The LowDown: Understanding Inflation: A Stop Motion Explainer." 2014. https://ca.pbslearningmedia.org/resource/mkqed-math-rp-inflation/understanding-inflation-stop-motion-explainer

Treebold, Jim. "Inflation and the Future Value of Money." March 31, 2018. https://www.encyclopedia.com/articles/inflation-and-the-future-value-of-money

Glossary

circulation (sur-kyuh-LAY-shuhn) money being passed from person to person

consumers (kuhn-SOO-murz) people who buy goods and services

deflation (dih-FLAY-shuhn) a decrease in the amount of available money or credit in an economy that causes prices to go down

demand (dih-MAND) the desire to purchase goods and services

embargo (em-BAHR-goh) a government order that limits trade in some way

exchange rate (iks-CHAYNJ rayt) a number that is used to calculate the difference in value between money from one country to another country

exports (EKS-ports) goods that are sold to another country; to export is to send goods to another country for purchase

imported (im-PORT-ed) brought in to buy from another country

index (IN-deks) a number that indicates changes in the level of something when it rises or falls

inflation (in-FLAY-shuhn) a continual increase in the price of goods and services

interest (IN-tur-ist) the money paid by a borrower for the use of borrowed money

raw materials (RAW meh-TEE-ree-uhlz) basic materials that can be used to make or create something

recession (rih-SESH-uhn) a period where there is less economic activity and a lot of people can't find jobs

supply (suh-PLY) the amount of something available to be used

taxes (TAKS-ez) an amount of money that a government requires citizens to pay that is used to fund the things the government provides for them

wages (WAYJ-ez) an amount of money that a worker is paid based on the time worked

Index